Praise for
Bloodlines

There is a call for remembrance in these poems, a call not to forget how generations survive, how they marry the land, marry their beloveds, and marry memory: "Remember that bloodline / Remember our blood," Bianca V. Gonzalez Perez writes, as if writing to her past and future self, as if writing to those who will come after. These poems are the bloodlines of the "[h]eart pulsing / [y]ears pulsing," an eternal familial pulse yearning to hold itself together. To love. And as Gonzalez Perez reminds us: love "is the relation between dead things, dying things, poisonous things." This is where love begins: in the knowing of what to kill and what to let go. Read these poems that want to see everything, which is another way to say that everything in them is a way to love the world.

—**Octavio Quintanilla**, author of
The Book of Wounded Sparrows (Texas Review Press)

Bloodlines is a beautifully articulate and vulnerable exploration of generational lineage set in a place of borders in the metaphysical and physical sense. In this way, Gonzalez-Perez does not shy away from the interrogation of the self, nor do her lines cower from commentary on societal structures that tear down legacies.

Bloodlines is very much a love letter to familial bonds and Texan borderlands. Her readers are lucky to see this love shown on every page, from start to finish.

—**Bianca Alyssa Pérez**, author of *GEMINI GOSPEL*

This radiant debut by Bianca V. Gonzalez Perez captured my heart. By turns blunt and lyrical, elegiac and sensual, the poems in *Bloodlines* trace the currents of individual passion against the backdrop of family history and the masculine intensity of border culture. "This is Texas, not heaven," the speaker writes, conjuring the violence and sweetness—the venomous snakes and the sugary figs—that commingle in this book's bend of the Rio Grande. Here we meet a speaker who is by turns a daughter, sister, lover, and expectant mother—who owns not only her cultural and familial inheritance but also, breathtakingly, her desires. By the end of this book, she has found her true self, an arrival that I can only describe as a luminous homecoming.

—**Cecily Parks**, author of *The Seeds*

Bloodlines by Bianca V. Gonzalez Perez asks: "Can you feel that?" and the answer is a resounding yes. This collection is viscerally felt, woven with snakes, grief, blood, memory, violence, rivers, family, and place. "This is Texas, not heaven. Nothing / more, nothing less," Gonzalez Perez writes, as we enter the searing heat of these poems, which radiate with startling imagery and precise form. This book is an excavation and Gonzalez Perez's poetry opens up questions of what we leave behind and what we return to, with familial ache and unflinching language: "Blood on knucklebones, creek beds, amber sap / all staring back at me." I keep returning to these poems again and again, blood-full and singing of wounds that can not be forgotten.

—**Jane Wong**, author of
Meet Me Tonight in Atlantic City

~~BLOODLINES~~

FLOWERSONG
PRESS

poems by

BIANCA V. GONZALEZ PEREZ

FLOWERSONG
PRESS

For my siblings,
Alexis and Ricky.

table of contents

I. LEAVING

II. RETURNING

We make a spoken pact to leave—
to leave it all behind
and never come back.

BLOODLINES

I.
LEAVING

"Come, little green snake. . ."

—Borderlands,
Gloria Anzaldúa

Our Blood

Held my breath
as I swallowed
bloodline; shed my self

Over and over again and
over and

My daughter organs now dense
with heme. You were breathless
at birth, have emerged
from death.

Brother, hold
this close— a final
lesson on heat.

Sunday Morning Breakfast with my Father on [redacted] Cocobolo Road, Del Rio, Texas.

Now that my father and I are older, now that we have more to say, it's always about the snakes: which snakes we saw that year, which ones we saw dying and dead on a fence, whose property, which brand of snake boots fit best. Love is the relation between dead things, dying things, poisonous things. His silence fits my silence. Generational. Eyes wide set. We map clues into each other. Into this isolation. We talk about the superficial, the unimportant, the masked. We watch television at breakfast underneath the flickering bulb lights and shelter from the heat. The popcorn ceiling is falling out. I can almost touch it with my fingertips. My father used to lift me with his heavy hands so I could watch the bubbling of the pancake batter on the stove. That's where I live. In memory. The small bend of Texas. We have always been this way. Now that I'm older, we talk about snakes, the dead ones he latched onto our fence line as a warning. To whoever is left. *I cut it in half,* he said, *then the head bit the body.* Then the fucking head bit the body. Can you feel that? Biting itself, the way we bite the edges of our skin, hang our nerves on fence lines, as proper warning. When we both run out of things to say, we stop speaking. I stand to open the blinds. Let the light in, wherever the head bites the body.

Heat Stain

The acid
will not seep thinly but rushes
into the dried creek with those
miracle water spiders, the riled
up collie, the mesquite dead from
thirst, the misplaced yucca and her bulbs.

We have this conversation. Often,
about snakes. It's my favorite
thing to talk about when we're
together. Me, Alexis, Ricky. Our story
begins here, when Ricky tells me to walk
ahead of him, we listen to the danger
of the grounded sizzle, his dog and her
bow-legedness jotting behind. The stone
of the old dogs' graves piled underneath the April overcast.

We make a spoken pact and promise to leave—
to leave it all behind and never come back. Let's save
ourselves already, from this land, this devastation,
the early memory of our uncle's suicide.
We can fill the snake holes with dirt,
give the dirt a blessing, go our way, rifles in hand.
Ricky hangs his head down like every old cowboy.

With specks of sun in the gaps of our teeth,
we couldn't know we were disappearing.

These are the lessons of heat.
In the body, in the rain, in the memory.
But I like talking about the snakes, because
after years of our conversations, I know
which to kill and which to let alone.

Because of Where We Live

This is Texas, not heaven. Nothing
more, nothing less.

The river is just blue.
No one knows how deep it is.

No one cares or no one cares
to ask.

I was young when I asked my father
how many souls are asleep at the
bottom.

These things happen,
you know—

These things happen,
you know—

I was young when I asked my father
how many souls are asleep at the
bottom.

No one cares or no ones cares
to ask.

The river is just blue.
no one knows how deep it is.

This is Texas, not heaven. Nothing
more, nothing less.

Because of where we live.

[redacted] Alderete Lane,
Del Rio, Texas

[In September 2021, more than 14,000
migrants camped on the U.S. side of the
Rio Grande under the Del Rio International
Bridge, waiting to open asylum claims with
Customs and Border Protection.]

If I could scratch the sky and paint it
some juvenile color,
I would catch the drone filming my house,
show my face, and the pot-hole edges
of Alderete Lane, something too illusive to believe,
an eye-witness account of where I am from.
For years I have been trying to write it down,
my house sitting on the edge of a crisis:

Fourteen-thousand migrants sleeping beneath the international bridge,
bomb threats eight-hundred feet away from me,
where my father has worked for fifteen years,
where he is probably reading a magazine, waiting
for a carton of prohibited mangoes to pass through,
or a truckload of heroin-infested wood to seize.
To the left: My tia Rosy watering the banana trees.
To the right: My mother telling me to come inside,
close the gate, *hurry,* even though there is no
lock, but because my father is not home, he's

800 feet away, and I can see Mexico
through my kitchen window. And my mother
sits alone inside with her daughters. I wanted to
go to college just to tell people that.

I see my house from a drone on KENS- 5 News,
          (I want to tell people that)
I see my cousin Gus, a Border Patrol agent,
on the front page of the *San Antonio Express*,
          (I want to tell people that)
I see no more water on the shelves in the grocery store,
yet we all are quenched,
in our tiny little homes, with our tiny little lives,
and the tiny little tv telling me the news,
and my tiny little mother telling me
it's wrong.

I see my brother, 5'10" and beautiful,
right back at where we come from:
This bloodstained desert, the Carrizo cane by the river,
slowly growing taller than him,
waiting for him to leave, then return,
and only bending their backs a little,
he's standing in the middle
of the University, twenty, young,
thumbs are green, and I want him to
tell me what he wants. Mostly I
want him to keep leaving. To keep not
coming back.

My cousin Gus, 6'0" and beautiful,
my neighbor for all my life,
I see him giving water from
his canteen to the little girl
in front of me, it is 98F, feels
like 115F, and he does not want to
leave this place, this way of life,
but I want him to.

The thing about growing up on the border
is it does not ask you
                    what you want,
what is given,
            is given to you.
I did not ask for bomb threats.
I did not ask to be able, to touch
the river water, and wash the salt
off my skin. It was given. It was
given.

I grew up with no fear about
the cartel barging into a local
restaurant, or that bomb sending
the maquiladoras up in flames.
I grew frozen, but all the moms,
all the same, lined outside at midday
to pick up their kids and take them home—
somewhere safe?

My friend from college said they heard gunfire
from the courtyard of their high school,

while the pledge of allegiance rang
through the young and hardened hearts
of theirValley. Another friend from Rio Grande City
said his friend's ex-girl was beheaded.

Who am I?
Who are we to go to the grocery stores
and come back everyday with nothing
being said, shared, lived, loved?
One tomato was bad, so we throw it away.
One cherry looks sweet, so we eat it
before washing.

Months later, I see my cousins drinking in their barn,
fires and beer and cold air burning
with the brush by the river.

I see my brother, grown, going
with them, looking to fix
what was given, still
leaving, always going.

[And though I don't agree with what they are
about to do next, my men come out late in the
night to the sparks flying above
the tin barrel, and they take their shotguns
and shoot them up
to the world.]

                                        Gone.

Knucklebones

After Anne Sexton

We drove to Ricky's new home,
The boonies, I told my husband,
Good thing the kid can fight.
Everything runs quiet, dangerous,
the threat of a dried river. Quail peck
at the barbed wire, we pour charcoal in the fire,
let flames highlight the dried buffalo grass,
fill the holes Dakota dug in the mud as she latched
her mouth onto my knucklebones, then running off,
like the back yard was her entire world. I raised
my fragile fist in the air, all green vein and blood
and told Ricky, *I told you she would do this.*

But the dog doesn't care. Her legs long and fawn-like,
she sits there in the shade, watching
my husband, watching
all of us watching what is
between the sky and dead
mesquite. The reflection of red
blood on my knucklebones.
I'm wondering how to be born
again, purified by this primal pain. It's almost
nothing.

Dakota's tongue hangs from thirst.
I watch her watching me, watching the sky.
Blood on knucklebones, creek beds, amber sap
all staring back at me.

You Died and Now I Know What Every Poem Means / San Ygnacio, Texas

For Gloria

I have been wanting to ask you
if the wind was warm as you were dying,
and I want you to know that your death
could not have been as tragic
as misplaced time, as your brother
Wayo's bright blue eyes brimmed to the sun
at the exit.

I wanted to ask you, as you pressed your lips
to the cursive of poems you must have loved,
if the poems spoke themselves in.
If the wind was warm as you were dying,
your neck bare with pride, chin up,
sun spots in all your glory,
grey hair I will never comb again,
if you were happy with this life.

I wanted to ask you what you wanted from me.
And I wanted to ask in agitation-
                    What do you want from me?
I still don't know.

    Is this it?

(The vine chain-linked to your old fence is in bloom. Wayo's blood has been scrubbed from the floor. The house sold. The rural town you came from is now a registered / sanctuary for butterflies. The devastated highway, where we saw Wayo, the one who looked beautiful and aged like Jesus, blue eyes beaming to the sun and hitchhiking, has not been cured, and, if you don't mind, what *was* your favorite poem, if you ever had one? I hope it was about the blue metalmarks / closing themselves into the earth.)

My Mother's Spring

Years after your brother Chuy was alive, and I was
stomach-flat on the grass and writing of roses,
either dead or bleeding, something
surrendered from you, vanished.

And we couldn't know it
        as you filled the watering can
        with hard metal showers for your
        new green peppers in the Spring.

You thought you could see me, hiding from the sunlight,
next to the dying dog, whom I didn't know was on
his last breath, and I, barefoot, middle of meadow,
no color save the contrast of brown dirt and horizon.

Now you know, I was a girl
        feeling in the fear of life,
        of the coming of motherhood.
        A fear I thought would always be
        a fear
        becomes a want.

These hands of mine were once your hands.

Your hands now beautiful, older, freckled,
worlds beneath the fingernails, the same ones
that bless me in the glow

of night, the cross-shape of your floating hands
between my temples.

The sleep I didn't know was coming.

Borders

We used to hate where we were from, the quietness of the house
we lived in, my sister and I. Now I stare at the pastures in front
of my parents home, the one that belongs to my grandparents.
The cows and the cows' white birds living in synergy. Unscathed
ecosystem in the palm of God's hand. I want nothing more than
to go back with my husband, build a tiny home, get a van, plant
a garden. The same garden bed as my mother's, four simple cherry
oak boards, nailed together by my father's numbing hands. Keep
it as memento. Watch the garden die someday, too.

My mother still holds my hands. While we watch movies, ride
in the old Ford, on our way to the ranch, those parched forty
acres where miracles of watermelon came into fruition. I am the
last daughter here. Look how my mother touches my face and
remembers her own. How she looks into my wide-set eyes and
sees her husband. To love like that.

Yes, I admit it. I have made my life out of the nakedness of
memory. Look at me, loom over me in the cold without clothes,
on the bed, tired. I let you marry me. I let you have me. Gladly,
panting, crying, God Bless— I love you. How human we are, the
way you stand taller than me, stronger than me, yet you look so
gentle, sitting near those Texas lantanas, all alone.

Self Among the Figs

I often wonder if peeling the orange
makes you feel strong, useful.

And when you use them, those carnal canines,
that overbite, those unremoved wisdom teeth,
if you feel more animal than ever.

                              Now bite.

An image I have of you, for softness:

     Your hair dangling below
     your knees, uncut for seven
     years, picking the figs, knowing
     Spanish for a lifetime,
     forgetting it, just the same.

You were a thin thing, a dying thing.
Everyone whispered around you. Your teeth
did not know the carnal crunching of the good
fruit.

But the Easter lilies kept blooming.
Did you look at them?

And the figs kept pumping their fat
sugars, like sweet crystals falling on your skin.

Did you look at the lilies? The ones
we brought back from the Valley?

They kept coming back.

Gloria's Hands Holding Beautiful Things

The smell of well
water and cinnamon.
Our hands kneading
flour and canned
carnation milk.

My hands you never
called beautiful,
but were yours,
always yours.

Memory of you scraping
dough off my fingers.
Your skin, older than mine,
weathered, so you could.

Memory of Alexis extending
her tiny hands. Alexis
looking at me. Alexis with
your blue eyes. Alexis with
your laugh.

The recipe still calls for
flour, canned milk, and
our hands. These hands

that you never called
beautiful, but are still
yours.

Listen

Even the hairs
on the stems
are remembering
you.

Breathe Me In My Post-American dirt
For Ricky

Point to where
it hurts. This is our dirt
and we knew it,
coddled beneath us
rusting our bones, magnetic deposition of
metal. We know dirt when we see
it.

I want the land to break me
over and over again. We're screaming
in the shed that was a coop,
a blood stain from a hen,
running and dead.

We know dirt when we see it.
Dirt that won't stop dividing, dirt
that won't stop crying, dirt I am
angry with, dirt I am born from, dirt
on the boots your lover spit on.

You are young, but you are rusting. Your
bloodline is fading, the mustang is running,
her blood oozing out. Your land has become
        a body, devalued. It, too, is fusing.

Unmask the guise of water.

the river wants to dry, it is crying—*dirt!*
It has spilled from our eyes. Like a child
lifting up my shirt, I point to where it hurts.

I knew it,
      my wounds are from this dirt.

II

There is a river
   It is running
I am running
   It is flowing
I am flowing
     It is drowning
I am drowning
     It is draining
I am draining
     It is dreaming
I am dreaming
     It's always a river
I'm always a river
     It can be something
Else
     I can be something
Else
     It is swimming
I am swimming
     It is lucid

I am lucid
　　It is becoming
I am becoming
　　And the water

III

Float.

I can feel more than I see,
in the cold crypt of night, your words
on the tongue, I forget
how the ground crunches when I step,
like heavy heavy heavy.
I feel that water and taste that water
and cleanse myself holy
　　enough
　　more
　　south, farther away from this
city, colossal collapse and a dust
storm.

Survive, if not for me, then for you,
Y-y-you
　　　　your

[Words will not come, water will not come,
dust will not come, eclipse will not sun]

So
    bloom

Where
on earth did you forget

I was always
the one trying to live.

Breathing.
Breathing.

A River Runs Through Blanco

Not that I was afraid of where
the road would take us. I knew

of the river that runs dry in that country
where every parched pebble is perfected

by weathering, and the dried
acid sap speaks us into sleep,

these are the certain things
I keep to hold my brother

and the yellow blooms of my city
wilt at the thought of his leaving.

I remember the image we have,
my arms stretched from East to west,

like a child I mumble, *the river is this big*,
same gap in my teeth, like Chuy. Innocent at best.

There is this conscious effort to surpass
it- the dryness, to hang my cross on

The dashboard of my brother's truck
driving through Blanco. I want

so badly to buckle the tape recorder
of my thoughts and speak in its endless

aim, static abyss of generated song,
running fast in spite of rain.

This First Time

for Daniel

I know this is big. I know this is adult of us.
Your grown body relaxed underneath the humid sun. We don't
talk. We sit. We ponder. You wonder if your hands work beneath
my warmth. They do.
I know this is big, burden, brown earth. My greens melting in a
metal bowl. We're laughing, naked underneath fresh garments,
olive oil in our hair,
picking at our scalps with fleshy digits and the scent of natural springs.
I know how scary it is, to watch the world loop
outside the kitchen window, to hear the heat
of highway in the night. The strangers opposite our walls. How
human we are in the quiet.
I release you in Barton Springs. Vulnerable as a berry seed on the
surface. Your eyes will not
let me go. I do this thing where I tilt my head back to the water
and wet my heavy hair.
We have moved through this life so young.
When you said *our children* for the first time, I was twenty-three.
As if there could be a womb in between my crooked pelvis, once
devalued and once devastated.
As if there was no more hurt in my spine.
As if your invisible hands held me in the remainder of that rough terrain.
As if to know, we will make love before you turn twenty-eight,
and you will whisper to me, *have my child, please.*
As if to say, *oh, how quickly we human ourselves, to learn each other
in this human way.*

[Fragments:

My thoughts are parentheses,
my heart beat acting like forever—

Three siblings sit under the sun,
open their mouths for water—

the creek
cracks in two—

The whole ground hard as unspoken esophagus
The whole red turned pink then white
The sun and her burn aligning
I know this dry storm flame lyre holy
spark—

Acid-stained leaf,
    gold quail eye in a
        tattered nest
These, my mediums—

The quail trailed your ankles in circles,
The land's first bleed—

My mother holds my sun-soaked
face in her hands

    I tell her

I am the same age
as you when you had me—

At the end of all this:

In the quiet air, there will always be nothing. We will always just be, as the olive sparrow in her quest, quiet, looking not to intrude, seeking always a perfect shelter.

]

II.
RETURNING

". . . let the wound by the serpent
be healed by the serpent."

—*Borderlands,*
Gloria Anzaldúa

Burial

When the cancer spread like thick
sap throughout my Tio Tavo's body,
and Ricky drove my mother and me to the ranch
to kill quail for him, because we heard it would heal
the sickness, I heard:

Boom
   Boom boom

Boom

   Boom

And the five quail shot dead by Ricky's hand plopped on their
sides.

I sat on the green canvas swing tied to an old
mesquite branch, and listened to the echo
of the gunshots. That was memory.

Ricky slung his twelve-gauge behind
his shoulder and walked toward those
big bellied birds, work gloves on, held their twig
legs between his fingers, and walked back to us.
Walked back to us with what seemed to be medicine.

I thought of my Tio Tavo resting in his rock home
by the river. I thought about how sick he must have felt.
How many tears my mother's mother shed.
And her daughter, and her granddaughter, and her grandson.
All hunting for something.

Ricky took the quail to the back of the truck.
He plucked the feathers.
He gutted their bellies.
Buried their warm insides into the dirt.

It's okay if the coyotes find the intestines, he said,
wiping the blood from the pocket knife onto his jeans,
there's no water here, anyway.

Her Body

Thirty-six centimeters under Lagloria loam,
her body bent. Her left arm as fragile
as it went, softly touching the
patella and her digits still
fusing into this dirt, becoming
Valley. After all these years.

I imagine the heat oppressive that day,
and the shine of the workers' hats
glossy in the sun's reflection. We enter
into the excavation: first the ancient horn shell,
then the ochre beads, a conch whorl pendant. Then her.

The report read no pathologies. A young,
Native American female.
No evident trauma.
All limbs intact, all organs absorbed
by bloodland. Fragile. Perhaps my age.
Perhaps in love. Perhaps alone.

As I flipped through the report, I understood
the poetry written in the science:
Her body was facing the Rio Grande.
That longing. Perched in the fetal position, strands
of hair still wrapped around her ankles.

When my mother tells me to run into the river,
I am twenty-seven. I am in love. I am alone. I am
about to bear children.

When I reach the water, I can barely stand to touch it.
My hair grows past my hips, wants to touch
my ankles. I find myself holding my own
knees with my hands. They keep getting thinner.

Beautiful Broken Inglish

It's the same sound every morning:
her pale feet on the sandstone floor,
the whole town quiet,
the stolen saguaro in a new coordinate.

This is aging, living, and dying.
All the babies have their own
babies, all her grandsons gone to war,
only the tapping quail run.

At age sixty, my father's grandmother began
her first English lesson at the Boy's Club.
When she writes to my childless father
in Ft. Benning, she writes with a thin hand:

Is my Inglish good?

She keeps writing.

No one cares about the sandstone,
the saguaro, the sugarcane leaning
against a broken fence line, and all the buffalo
grass this land could ever carry.

Forty years later, my father visits San Ygnacio again.
He points to a white house.
Even the cracks exposing the stone are beautiful.

That's where my grandma lived, he said,
we only spoke Spanish in that home.

Cenchuras

*"If I say, My river is disappearing, do I also mean My people
are disappearing?"*

—Natalie Diaz

I break a promise with the land

and crawl back. I could not be helped.

I smile while the sun makes a home

on the spine of my crooked neck.

I know this border valley heat.

Was born by it and into it.

And so was my father.

And all the father's fathers.

I am his daughter.

I can admit that now.

I crawl back into the river's mouth.

Turn my head to what once
                    was river.

I've always known this:

    Warm blaze of buffalo grass,

    beating of a daughter heart.

I am no myth breaker.

I fuse with this mouth.

Nothing could stop me.

The Clouds Like My Dreams Remain Countless

The world could have burned at Chuy's funeral:
> Black, grey, smeared
> tar on his daughter's face
Picture it: rain, tears, grass
> stained on the windows of his closed
> irises, and everyone else's eyes-
> opened.

I have this dream where I'm there,
eating a sugar cookie before it happened.
I'm looking at you, my mother's brother,
the laugh spilling from your mouth.

I cannot hear you.
I stop the dream.

The dream is recurrent. I am afraid to ask
if the dream is real. I ask the air and it does
not answer.

Decades like thousands of days
have passed, and we still hear you
in the purples of the sage.

The one and only king for miles.

From Beyond the Desert Realms

Remember the air of this
Remember the sage and their dance
The quail and their industrious song
Remember the cancers of heat and flame
Remember the water
Remember the dirt (*the dirt the dirt the dirt*)
Remember the scorched land and her fawn
Remember the wretchedness of stone beneath bare feet
Remember unafraid
Remember undead
Remember divided
Remember Wayo's arms lifted, eyes illuminated
Remember seeing until never unseeing
Remember our mother's soft hands
Remember eyes on the peaks of Mexican mountains
Remember your birth in a ford of water
Remember the name of time as gasoline
Remember those wide-set eyes of the forgotten son
Remember the light of the next day claiming you
Remember the dust trail behind you
      scattering gravel and what our father told you
Remember the mercy of generational
      suicide and our bloodline begging you to survive
Remember that bloodline
Remember our blood

Remember our sister
      how she only calls for us from beyond the desert realms
Remember the wars before us, the wars apart us, the wars after us
      our hands stained from shed we can't remove
      from land that only wanted to tear us apart?

I want to feel it now.

Remember what it meant to be

                    still.

Hello / Goodbye

Not that the whirring of the land
wasn't exquisite
wasn't white
wasn't it

                quiet
in its own scorch

Didn't it feed in its
own parch

Now, aren't we
reborn, aren't we

My face the same
your face the same
as my face

The tongue in my cheek
is as
they like it
licked slick

                back

And all the snakes

                    sisters
                    brothers

blisters

My child
My womb
      aches
For a child
 (I said it
To the land

Watching

(Patience

              God was watching God.)

Doesn't It Scare Me

Heat of the land
Heat of the body
Soundscape heavy
Metal of bone heavy
In the sun that wanted
To be nothing but
A cold vein wrapping
Itself around sky pulsing
Everything pulsing
Sound pulsing
Heart pulsing
Years pulsing
There
is a drought
You have felt long
Before we were
Born
Same land
Same invisible
Body same
Excavation
Our home map
All of it
Archaeological
All of it

Bursting because
Bursting in flame
Meant heaven because
Heaven meant two
Eyes stuck on the
sparks forward, in front,
forward, no less.

Running on a Graveyard

Grief looked like

                                 excavation

               like

Missing is always part

Of the ubiquity I

Play part

     in, in all my lives in
All worries, woes, di-

Mensions

Is this, the world

     you leave me on-
Is this

          the last time

The small

        of my larynx

Mimics   your voice

Could it be this

Grief

    looking like

            excavation?

           You

Giving it a Name

I love the way the light means. In that gorgeous dark-indigo dark.
Native eyes. The way the light means on my skin. Offspring of
poverty. Where are your eyes from. My blood runs thick in this
scorch. My blood runs thick the way Wayo once ran down the
corridor. My father cried while he smiled. Heard my heart through
a poem said I heard the river in your poem. Wayo stood in the river
one last time at the exit. Remembered smiling when I was born. He
remembered it. Held me and his mind was already gone. Smiled
while he cried. Standing at the exit. In the river. The very last time.
I said I'm happy for you, Tio. Cried while I smiled. Walked waist-
deep to meet him in the river. Cried while I smiled. The light
beaming into skin. He smiled. Raised his arms and looked up to the
Lord said Jesucristo ya no tengo nada. Ya usé todo lo que me diste.
Turned his eyes down to himself. And the water. Blood dripping
from the wound. The Lord looked at him said well done my good
and faithful servant. I cried because I was there meet me where that
first cut runs. I keep running. Through the blaze of buffalo grass.
Our weathered hands. Just enough first blood to become the story.
I can't even bring myself to closure. To hold the hands that hold
me. To give this story a name. So call it what it wants to be called.

Sinkhole as Shelter

This is my handed down body. If I told God:

I could live this way forever, eternity symbol bumper stickers
and my headlights with the battery on.

I'd say I could still see my fingers lightly turning the steering wheel

and I could catch God

if I wanted to to.

But I have played too much of that story
in my head.
Too many conversations.
Too many of the same fucking snakes.

 Apart. In bed. Coalesce. Running to

Some imparted future where I no longer
exist.

But I can see it, this end, this thirst enervating deep in the bones
to touch

My motion sickness, deep in those wicked ways. I still become a
snake. I curse, I bleed, I burn, I come back, I bloom. Forgiven. I
forgive you.

Running Fast in Spite of Rain

Beginning of desert

is

    the ending of valley
is

    the old pecan orchard.

is

    the birth of my mother.

    And her sisters.

    And her brothers.

Midday. All the

    little bodies, lined in a row of life.

The Deer

For Gerardo and Adelina Gonzalez. After Ada Limón.

I

The rocks make their marks
on me. I bear them, and as two
white-tipped doves fly in their lines, southern-
bound with velvet coats / the story opens.

The Kickapoo say a white-
tailed deer is given seven lives.

My father has explained this killing
of a deer twice:

                  Don't feel bad. Seven lives.

II

I remember all the lives inside me.

We open the sky in the mouth of the river.

Two people: a man and a woman,
          on opposite sides of the mouth.

One of them is speaking. The other
cannot hear.

They are saying they are in love. They are saying
the water will burn them. They say,

Come to me through the mouth of this river.

Their own lips fuse shut.

Jujubes reach fruiting.
The water stops moving
so fast. The man and woman
are naked. And the deer—

III.

It's a fiction I want to believe in.

But it's fiction that won't move me.

Because my great-grandmother waited,
on her side of the mouth, and instead of falling in,
she stood six-feet tall and unafraid,
like the saguaro in a stolen coordinate.

Because meeting in the river was genesis.
And I'm sure the tears she shed as she watched
the man who would become her husband
cross that torrent moved her to tears which ran so long they

live inside me now.

His face never goes away.
His eyes squinting under the sun's beam
and the limestone cutting the skin of his mestizo feet
and the blood that soaked
the grass beneath her as he crawled out of the mouth.

Never having lost a single life.

IV.

It would be a beautiful story if the story
ended there.

But it keeps coming back to me.

I'm with the deer. The rocks making their marks on me.

A perfect shot,

My father says, as one life gone swings from dead

mesquite, it's tongue purple and nervous, it's teeth
totem-like, small workings of ancient stone.

My father has been using the same pocket knife for years,
and that first cut always runs deep.

I stand to touch the hide,
the heart, the liver, lungs,
warm and wild.

I was sixteen when my iris beamed
through the lined scope of a rifle. With mine own eye
I followed that creature straight into its calling.

Held my breath as I swallowed bloodline.

V.

I wonder where the deer and I will meet next.

Perhaps somewhere in Spring
Branch, captured among bluebonnets, wild
onions, fearless, proud of knowing where it's been,
and where it's going. Its last earthly sight on two
white-tipped doves, encircling the final sacrament.

But I know this world better.
I know the sacrifices made over rivers, water

so loud it drowns the voice, or becomes it.
And the only option left

    is to cross.

I know the deer that roam
this earth, their lives like coins I get to choose.

Blood so close.

"How I love this tragic valley. . ."

—Borderlands,
Gloria Anzaldùa

Bloodlines

For Manuel de Jesus Flores Martinez

> *"Out of poverty, poetry,*
> *Out of suffering, song"*
> *—Mexican poem*

~~I could not deny— this writing of remembrance—~~the most
important thing— pecan trees. All one-hundred and thirty-seven
of them— sturdy and fearsome— I won't forget— to tell you I
once labored— before bras before sex— before—we learned to
dance— around the wound— may these words—wounds— cast
out grief— for a short time—as seen in old family film— heart
ties— so what if I'm misplacing grief? A yellow— FOR SALE—
sign hangs around the pecan orchard— wants to fall from a
fence— mended by Chuy's hands— my mother's cell phone
number is on it— each time someone calls to ask— how much
the land of my childhood is worth— she raises the price— a
little more— a little more— a little more— my hands picked—
pecans— Chuy should have shipped— to Quemado— near the
birthplace of my husband— this is how—the world breaks—my
grandfather paid me— two American dollars every time— I look
still— at the pecan trees— they have started— to look like him—
dark foreign full— of lines— blue green irises wide— resist
shutting— I am proud of my grandfather and the bark of the
trees— because they are dark jagged unafraid— but his feet— are
white he is— unashamed of how this world has worked him—

this is the orchard— where the land breathed and my brother began— we are each a tree— mine is green fragile wracked— pecans fall from me like— bloodline we are— bloodlined in rows— I carry the light and dark of my people who came before me— and the unborn child I now carry within me— and I am unafraid.

Notes

"[redacted] Alderete Lane"

    This poem was originally published in *Juke Joint Magazine* for their 11th volume, Summer 2022, which has, for reasons unknown, since been taken down, This is possibly due to the poem's nature of illegal immigration, my father's government affiliation, and/or firearm use. Documentation section was extracted from *El Paso Times*, and can be found at: https://www.elpasotimes.com/story/news/2021/11/30/ del-rio-texas-haitian-migrant-crisis-acuna-timeline-news- coverage/8639273002/.

"Love is the Relation Between Dying Things"

    The title of this poem is excerpted from a line by writer and philosopher, Sir Roger Scruton, and can be found at: https://unherd.com/2022/01/what-true-conservatism- looks-like/#:~:text=%E2%80%9CLove%20is%20a%20 relationship%20between,mortal%20and%20will%20 pass%20away.

"Her Body"

    This poem comes after reading a report about an accidental excavation in San Ygnacio, Texas 1991, in front of a relative's historic home. Original line as noted in the report is excerpted from *Exhumation at 41ZP144, Zapata County,* https://rrpress. utsa.edu/items/8f460654-b9a8-4487-987d-897ea4d840f4:

"The burial, located near the center of Trevino Street (San Ygnacio, Texas) immediately north of the intersection of Trevino Street and Washington Avenue, was uncovered 36cm below the paved road surface. It was laying on its left side in a loosely flexed position and was oriented on a north-south axis. The right arm was outstretched along the side of the body with the distal end of the lower arm near the pelvis. Although all but a fragment of the occipital was missing from the skull, it appears that the head was facing west, towards the Rio Grande River" (Munoz, 2013).

"Cenchuras"

The epigraph for this poem was excerpted from:

Postcolonial Love Poem, "The First Water is The Body", by Natalie Diaz. Scientific name for Buffalo Grass Extracted from a document by Texas A&M AgriLife Extensions, *Know Your Grasses:* https://leon.agrilife.org/files/2022/05/Know-Your-Grasses.pdf.

"Sinkhole as Shelter"

Title is a subtitle extracted from an anthropological report, "The Site and its Setting", *Plains:* https://www.tandfonline.com/doi/pdf/10.1080/2052546.1988.11909458. Original subtitle used: "Sinkholes Used as Shelters".

Acknowledgments

My sincerest gratitude to the keepers of these stories, those who came before me. To my parents, whom despite my offbeat path never discouraged me from writing or being my most authentic self. Thank you for creating a story teller. For loving me as, perhaps, your most complicated child. Thank you to my siblings, Alexis and Ricky, whose fierce spirits sparked the idea for this collection. Your ruggedness, your glamour, your tattoos, your rodeos, your red dirt songs playing on repeat, and the ranch we so dearly love is now weathered and parched but still stands. After drilling 476 feet, the drillers found no water left in the well. I cried like a child in a café in Austin as I thought my childhood had run dry, one in which our grandmother taught us to raise chickens and rabbits and goats, taught us to plant a garden North to South, how to sift flour for bread, and how to wash clothes by hand. These memories are where the poems began. Many times, these memories and poems were difficult to write, even more so to read aloud. Many times I did not want to remember what our bloodline has endured. But I'm grateful I did. That we do remember.

Thank you to my colleagues and mentors at Texas State University and Texas Lutheran University. Thank you, thank you, thank you, Dr. Cecily Parks, for your encouragement, your creativity, and being an absolute inspiration to all who cross your path. Many of these poems would not have made it to their final destination if it wasn't for your gentle guidance. Thank you for nurturing the "wild-ness" of these poems while encouraging my creative control.

Thank you to my poet twin, Bianca Alyssa Powell-Perez, author of *Gemini Gospel*. How grateful I am that the universe conspired to bring us into friendship. Poets in this world are rare. Having one who shares your name, interests, and birth week is even more rare. Thank you for your friendship, mentorship, and support. You've given me wonderful opportunities in the writing world and I deeply appreciate every one of them.

Thank you to William Jensen, Department Chair of Southwestern Studies at Texas State University, for serving on my thesis committee for 'BLOODLINES', for believing in this manuscript and encouraging me to contribute to Borderland poetics. Your classes were inspirational to the aesthetics and framework of this collection.

Special thanks to Dr. Octavio Quintanilla, Jane Wong, Dr. Sara Ramirez, Dr. Debra Monroe, and Cyrus Cassells whose mentorship and instruction built 'BLOODLINES' into the meaningful collection it is today. I have learned much about being a writer from each of you.

A very special thanks to FlowerSong Press, to my publisher Edward Vidaurre and production editor Avery Castillo. When I met the FlowerSong Press team at the Rio Grande Valley International Poetry Festival, I immediately knew there was a niche of poetry in which I belonged. Everyone at FlowerSong Press has made my work feel seen and important, which really, are the stories of my family. Thank you for making us feel seen. Thank you for this wonderful opportunity. I am forever grateful for this collection landing in the right hands.

Most importantly, thank you to my husband, Daniel. My dreams have come true because of you. Your growth has been a driving force for my own spiritual and intellectual development. Everyone saw how brave and free I became when you returned into my life. I would not be as courageous as I am today without you. For three years during graduate school, you observed me writing from every light and every angle, at strange hours, in random cafés, and you welcomed the poems time and time again. You saw the deep grief and immense joy as I spoke the words ("downloads") no one had ever heard before. You remained curious about every word and line, and you taught me to not be afraid of what the poems were telling me. You saw me transform from an adolescent to an adult writer, wife, mother, and healthcare worker. You are the witness to me becoming everything I have ever dreamt of being, and I hope this collection makes you proud. Since completing this manuscript, I have not written another poem, but I know the words will come again soon. As I write this, I am seven months pregnant with our first child, a son. Your bloodline within me. I love you more every second of it.

About the Author

Bianca V. Gonzalez Perez received her M.F.A. from Texas State University in 2024. Her debut poetry collection, Pouring Poetry was published in 2020 by Austin Macauley, LTD. *Bloodlines* was listed as a Semifinalist for *Sundress Publications*. Perez's work has been featured in *Juke Joint Magazine*, *Defunct Magazine*, *Morning Fruit*, *Harness Magazine*, and *Poet's Garden Alchemist*. She was born and raised in Del Rio, Texas, and writes ardently about West Texas and Borderland experience. *Bloodlines* was her thesis in graduate school, under the direction of award-winning poet Cecily Parks. The collection analyzes recollection, reconstruction of narrative, and cyclical trauma. Perez has an extensive background in health sciences as an undergraduate at The University of Texas at San Antonio. Perez switched her major to English Literature after four years of Pre-Med to explore her writing in depth. After obtaining her English degrees and teaching at the university level, Perez is now enrolled at UT Arlington to receive her Second Bachelor's Degree in Nursing, to reestablish her primary mission of serving the community and studying medicine. Perez currently lives in Austin, Texas with her husband, a registered nurse and avid reader, and the two are expecting their first child together. When not thinking about her next poem, Perez is outside exercising, reading nutrition books, cooking, or studying for her classes. You can find her on Instagram @biancavanessa_poet.

FLOWERSONG
PRESS

FlowerSong Press nurtures essential verse
from, about, and throughout the borderlands.
Literary. Lyrical. Boundless.

Sign up for announcements about
new and upcoming titles at:

www.flowersongpress.com